STRIKE THAT

Forget What You Think You Know about Paralegals

JAQUETTA R. BAZIER

STRIKE THAT

Forget What You Think You Know about Paralegals

Cover design by: Joshua Jadon

Author's photo by: Kaleb Fulk

Formatted by Frostbite Publishing

ISBN 978-0-692-94919-1

Printed in the United States of America

Pinnacle Litigation Connections, LLC

8190 Barker Cypress Road, #209

Cypress, TX 77433

www.pinnaclelitigationconnections.com

Request speaking engagements and bulk orders by contacting the author and publisher via email at: SupportMe@pinnaclelitigationconnections.com.

CONTENTS

INTRODUCTION

I REALLY HATE TO START THIS BOOK OFF ON THIS NOTE, BUT those of you who know my no-nonsense personality, know that I wouldn't have it any other way. A decade of working in law firms and with lawyers has been an eye-opener on how the legal industry operates. I've come to realize that legal support professionals, such as paralegals, are trained to work with lawyers, but lawyers know nothing about the art of working with paralegals and other legal support staff. Working with paralegals and other legal support staff is an art. It requires technique.

During my two years of paralegal education at the University of Oklahoma's School of Law, I learned how to be a true paralegal, not some notion people have created in their minds. I gained a deeper understanding about what it takes to truly support lawyers. Eventually, I began to think like a lawyer. I was taught to analyze the law, write briefs, draft discovery documents, and review records. I was taught to interpret words the way the court would interpret them instead of the definition of the same word in society.

The reason I obtained a paralegal education was to gain knowledge of the meat and potatoes of the practice of law—the why and the how. I wanted to be a self-starter. I didn't want to be micromanaged and have my hand held each and every step of the way in the legal process. Instead, I wanted to know why something was being done. More importantly, I wanted to know the purpose of each and every task. Purpose is important to me, and I believe that everything on this earth has its purpose. I wanted to be able to be five steps ahead of my attorney and get things done on my own. Armed with the why and the how, I became a greater asset to the legal industry and an extension of the attorney I was assigned to support.

Now that I operate a legal support firm that offers virtual paralegal and legal administrative assistant solutions to modern-day solo attorneys and small law firms, I am able to apply the why and the how in my goal of helping lawyers solve their problem(s), making their job easier by reducing stress, taking a load off them, and giving them their time back, all while increasing their bottom line. The majority of my attorney-clients are public speakers and teachers. They speak at events and workshops, they help other attorneys, and they are on social media teaching small business owners and entrepreneurs. What some people don't understand is that attorneys are entrepreneurs themselves. So, you may ask, while my attorney-clients are out in the trenches for their clients, who is on the front line for them? That would be me.

My name is Jaquetta Bazier. To most people, I am known as J. I am the founder of Pinnacle Litigation Connections, LLC, a small, minority, woman-owned, legal support company comprised of virtual paralegals, legal administrative assistants and consultants that work alongside you to effectively manage your time so you can generate profits for your law firm. We are known as The Attorney's Best Friend on social media.

My personal mission is to help you understand the role of paralegals and teach you how to properly utilize and incorporate the paralegal position within your law practice. I hope you enjoy this resource and rely on it continuously to bring balance and harmony to your professional life as an attorney.

If you're a young attorney venturing out on your own, congratulations! If you're already in practice, it's never too late to learn! With all of the technological advances taking place in the legal industry, now is perfect the time for you to learn all you can about working with one of the most important support roles in the legal industry: the paralegal.

Without adequate legal support, you're gambling with your time and your money.

Jaquetta "J" Bazier

❦ I ❧

J'S TAKE ON LAW PRACTICE
MANAGEMENT

"Great vision without great people is irrelevant."

— JAMES C. COLLINS

WHAT ARE THE FIRST THREE WORDS THAT COME TO YOUR mind when you think of law practice management? You may think of the software it takes to run your firm. What about the processes and procedures that need to be in place? Maybe you thought about the financial and marketing aspects of efficiently running your firm.

These are all great answers because each of those aspects play a significant role in operating a successful, profitable law practice. However, in any business, law firms included, people are the greatest resource. They are the foundation for your law practice. Without people, you have no business. Think about this oldie but goodie phrase, "The house is only as strong as it's foundation." Take some time and think about the people you have in place in your firm. How strong is your foundation?

Oftentimes, the people placed in position to effectively operate a law firm are overshadowed by the talk of the latest and greatest billing and client management software. Why? Because firm personnel are always on the bottom of the totem pole. Truth be told, people or firm personnel should always be a priority when it comes to managing a law practice, and I'll tell you why.

Firm personnel can keep your firm out of the red. Firm personnel can increase your profit margin. Firm personnel can free up your time to focus on other pertinent matters inside or outside of your law practice. Firm personnel can bring in more clients. Am I getting through to you yet? You're still scratching your head? I understand some people are visual learners, so let me try a different approach.

Grab a pen and a piece of paper and draw a tabletop. On this tabletop, I want you to place your law firm by drawing a picture of your firm (or writing your firm's name) on the table. Include all your resources such as the financials, the software you currently use, the technology and even your clients. Include any assets your firm has. What about intellectual property? Fill up your table. See how your tabletop is becoming overloaded? It cannot hold all the weight of the firm. What does the tabletop need for sustainability? What is needed to support all the weight? The tabletop needs legs!

In this analogy, the tabletop represents you, the attorney/law firm. The legs represent the support staff or firm personnel, such as paralegals. Did you notice how the tabletop was easily overloaded without the support or "legs" it needed? This happens to you when you attempt to do everything on your own while managing your law practice. Here's a newsflash for you:

You were not created to do each and every task on your own.

How can you focus on providing high-quality legal services to your customers if you're performing each of those tasks and wearing all of the hats? How can you generate profits if you're spending time scanning documents or sending out invoices at the end of the month? You can't. If you're spending 3 hours each day on the phone giving away free advice, you're losing money. You can't operate this way. This is why certain positions were created to support you. That's what those "legs" are for.

This is where you have your aha moment.

Allow me to describe the four "legs" that were created to support you and help run your firm like a well-oiled machine. Those "legs" are paralegals/legal assistants, legal secretaries, legal administrators/office managers, and legal receptionists. Please be advised that the above-mentioned may not be the complete level of support needed for your firm.

There are other positions, such as IT, marketing, investigators, etc., that may or may not be needed at your firm. Just make sure you plan, adjust and retain the right people for your law practice management structure accordingly to ensure you are not overwhelmed and overloaded, much like what happened with your imaginary table.

WHAT IS LAW PRACTICE MANAGEMENT ANYWAY?

Simply put, law practice management is the management of a law-related business such as a law firm or corporate legal department. The management of a law practice involves personnel, processes, procedures, marketing, financials, and technology.

The American Bar Association, along with other bar associations across the United States, places a keen focus on law practice management by developing divisions and programs to assist attorneys in this area, because becoming an attorney is like ordering a combo at a fast food burger restaurant. You order your J.D (burger)., you get your bar license (drink) and then throw in the business of a law practice on the side (fries). This concept applies whether you're flying solo or whether you're an associate in a firm.

Seriously, take a moment to think about this. You spent four years in law school learning only techniques, concepts, how to do legal research, write briefs and formulate legal arguments. When you took the bar and got your license, you thought to yourself, "I need to get a job." Once you got that job and eventually decided to strike out on your own, this is when you threw yourself into a totally different world -- the business aspect of running a law practice. At this point, you're no longer just a lawyer. You're a business owner *and* a lawyer. You were prepared for how to be a lawyer, but the latter one, running a business, i.e., law practice, was not something you were prepared to do.

The American Bar Association (ABA) was the first organization to focus on law practice management through its Law Practice Division, which was created in 1957. For many years, you've probably been getting help with resources to run your law practice. There are CLEs, webinars, books and events to help you with managing your law practice. You may even have a mentor—someone you admire and look up to. But if you have not checked out the ABA and its Law Practice Division, I highly recommend you do so. Also, check out your local bar association to see if it has a law practice management program. You just may be missing out on some valuable information right in your backyard.

I remember when I discovered the law practice management program at my local bar association. I was working at a law firm as a legal assistant in Oklahoma City in 2011 and learned about the Oklahoma Bar Association's Management Assistance Program while attending paralegal school in my law practice management class. A couple of years later, I ended up meeting the advisor of that program through my ethics teacher.

I was intrigued by the program because I had been observant throughout my paralegal career and took note of the areas that attorneys and law firms needed help with the most. They needed help with going paperless, file retention, and staying up to date on technology. Rarely did I see a discussion about understanding the roles of support personnel. This brings me to my mission today to help you understand these roles and to show you how to properly utilize them in order to run a successful law practice.

WHAT DOES LEGAL SUPPORT STAFF HAVE TO DO WITH MANAGING MY LAW PRACTICE?

Everything. As mentioned before, people or personnel will be your greatest assets in your law firm. Have you ever heard the saying, "Behind every great lawyer, there is a great paralegal"?

I would say this is an accurate statement. When it comes to your law practice, the people you hire or retain, whether employees or contractors, are important assets in law practice management.

These are the people who may come into contact with your prospective clients first. They may conduct initial intake interviews, they may be the ones ensuring your lawsuits are filed in a timely manner, they may be the ones to clean up your document that's full of typos, they may be the ones issuing payments to your vendors and they may just have better knowledge of the ins and outs of your office. If you don't know how to manage these people within your law practice, you can't possibly get the most out of them. Let's quickly get you up to speed on how to get the most out of your legal team.

"When you encourage others, you in the process are encouraged because you're making a commitment and difference in that person's life. Encouragement really does make a difference."

— ZIG ZIGLAR

HOW TO GET THE MOST OUT OF YOUR LEGAL TEAM

If you're a solo practitioner, eventually you will seek the services of others to help you reach your goals. If you're already in law firm management or leadership where you have to work with a legal team, you may realize you have a wonderful legal staff, but you struggle with how to get the most from them. First, you must change your way of thinking. Embrace the many talents your staff members bring to the table because without them, your business would not thrive. There are three simple ways to get the most from your staff.

Empower Them. Stop letting your staff come into your office day in and day out without giving them some sort of inspiration for wanting to be there. For some people, work goes far beyond getting a paycheck. Some people are looking to enhance and build their skills and some are looking for growth. Your staff is your greatest asset and they should be treated as such. Send them to conferences, seminars, and classes. Invest in your staff and they will be a greater benefit to your law firm.

Be Transparent. Let your intentions and goals be known up front with each and every staff member. Doing so will get your staff on board with your vision, and as a result, they will be eager to help you. Your staff can only help you as much as you are willing to let them help you. Have weekly meetings to disseminate information and have one-on-one conversations to see what your staff members are thinking. They usually have better insight as to what is going on in the office because they handle your daily duties.

Get Out of Their Way. This is probably the most important of all. Obviously, you hired this person because of what they can do for your organization. Let their contributions speak for themselves and do not micromanage. Remember, you hired people who are better at doing things you're not. Encourage them and let them know they are doing a good job. They deserve it.

Once you have a better understanding of the roles of the legal support staff, only then should you incorporate them into your law practice. Unfortunately, most attorneys incorporate these positions without having full knowledge of what these roles entail and what key positions they play in a law firm. Until you come to terms and have a complete understanding of the legal support staff, you, my friend, are functioning in chaos.

❧ 2 ❧

LAW PRACTICE CHAOS

"There's chaos out there, and chaos means opportunity."

— MARK OSTROFSKY

AFTER GETTING A MOUTHFUL ABOUT HOW YOU NEED TO understand the role of each legal support staff member, you may be wondering, "How am I functioning in chaos when I already have the staff you mentioned in place?" It's great that you have those people in place to help you. But the question is, *how* are their roles being applied in your law practice? Are you utilizing each position in the capacity of which it was created?

Just because you have those positions in place at your firm, does not mean that you *know* how they are to be utilized. How would you know? This is not something that is taught in law school. Because you are not properly utilizing each position, which make up the elements of the law practice, you are functioning in chaos.

Throughout my paralegal tenure, I've witnessed several instances where attorneys have unintentionally misused certain support staff roles. It's not that they are misusing these roles on purpose. It's that they haven't been taught *how* to properly utilize these roles. If you've never used the gas pump to put gas in your car, how would you know how to pump the gas?

All roles of the legal support staff have been misunderstood in some form or fashion. It's up to people like me and those you've hired to support you to show you how to use us in the manner in which we were created. You have to be open-minded and be ready to receive the knowledge we can pass on to you, just as we receive the knowledge you pass on to us.

The relationship between you and your support staff is one of mutual benefit. Some like to call it a win-win. Always keep in mind that you will not be the only one who can drop what I like to call "gold nuggets" of wisdom. You have to sit back sometimes and allow us to drop some of our gold nuggets on you as well. The relationship between an attorney and a legal support professional is give and take, and it is a two-way street. Since it is a two-way street, please do not dominate our lane because we couldn't possibly dominate yours.

Now that you understand you may be functioning in chaos by using your legal support staff in the wrong capacity, your question may be, "What can I do to fix this?" I'm glad you asked. This will be easier than you think. The good part is that you're never too old to learn something new, even if that something was under your nose the entire time.

FIXING THE HOT MESS

Again, you had no idea you were working in chaos. You had no idea your law practice was a hot mess. Oh, but I bet your paralegal, your legal administrative assistant, your receptionist and your office manager knew. There is no way you could have made this observation. You weren't taught to look for those clues in law school. You weren't taught how to run your law-related business. You weren't taught how to be present in the moment. You are too busy trading your time for money because your time is your money. You have to be choosy with how you spend your time. Jim Rohn said, "Days are expensive. When you spend a day, you have one less day to spend, so make sure you spend each one wisely."

You must be diligent in your use of your legal support staff. You wouldn't hire a plumber to landscape your yard, would you? No, you wouldn't. Your best solution to this problem is to thoroughly evaluate the positions in your office, determine what your needs are and use the positions for the reasons they were created. What do I mean? Well, let your receptionist answer the phone and handle incoming guests at the office. Allow your legal administrative assistant to type your letters and help with workflow. Let your office manager manage the office. Make room for your paralegal to serve as an extension of you in the areas such as research, analysis and legal writing so you can focus on what you do best: practicing law.

Now that you know how you got into this mess, it's time to discuss how to get out of it. This may take you some time to digest, but when you are in total agreeance with me, it will make your work life a little easier day by day. Based on my experiences, I believe there are three ways to fix the chaos in your law practice:

(1) Understand that you must utilize each legal support role properly;

(2) Know that your legal support staff are: trained professionals; and

(3) Give them the opportunity to do what they were created to do.

Oh, and let me add that these three need to be done in this order. If you ignore the fact that you need to understand that you must use each role properly, you can't know that those in the role are trained and finally, you can't give them the opportunity to do what they were created to do. Understanding, knowing, and giving (UKG) are the key elements you need to master when working with your legal support staff to fix the chaos in your law practice.

What you may not realize is that these positions were created with a purpose to benefit you. Each of these positions play their own unique roles in a law practice. They were created to work alongside you to accomplish your goal of providing excellent legal service to your customers. Paralegals are legal professionals who have been trained and educated to provide support to you. The same can be said for legal administrative assistants and the rest of the legal support staff.

The only difference between you going to law school and a member of your legal support staff going to their respective schools for training is the fact that they are taught to work with you. They are taught to support you. They get certifications, certificates and attend CLEs to provide the best support just for you.

Think about your days in law school. Nothing was mentioned about legal support staff. Nothing was mentioned about the ins and outs of running a law practice. You were taught to write briefs and memos, how to analyze the law and formulate arguments and strategies. You didn't find out about the legal support staff until you've actually stepped foot into a law firm where you learned processes and procedures by who? A paralegal.

THE NEED FOR THE PARALEGAL PROFESSION

For you to understand the role of the paralegal, you have to understand the history of the paralegal profession and why it was created. Believe it or not, the paralegal profession is relatively new. In fact, there are some lawyers who remember the time when paralegals didn't even exist.

The role of the paralegal wasn't created until the late 1960s. According to the National Association of Legal Assistants (NALA), the paralegal career began to develop when law firms and individual practitioners sought ways to improve the efficient and cost-effective delivery of legal services. The paralegal profession was created to assist attorneys with their caseloads. The profession was also created to help attorneys increase access to legal services.

As you can see, the paralegal profession was created out of necessity. It was necessary for attorneys to have help with their caseloads *and* help with spreading the access to legal services to underserved communities. I believe we are singing this same song today in 2017. The access-to-justice gap is just as wide now than ever before. This necessity resulted in the development of the paralegal profession. Actually, the first paralegal was a legal secretary who was trained OJT (on the job) to perform substantive legal tasks, usually performed by an attorney, under the direction of an attorney.

In 1968, the ABA formally recognized the paralegal

profession and since then, the paralegal profession has exploded into one of the fastest-growing job markets in the U.S. today. The U.S. Bureau of Labor Statistics states that the paralegal profession is projected to grow 8 percent from 2014 to 2024, as fast as average for all occupations.

PARALEGAL OR LEGAL ASSISTANT?

Let me make it clear that today's paralegal is not an administrative assistant. Today's paralegal is not even a legal secretary. I cringe every time I hear an attorney refer to their paralegal as their legal secretary or vice versa. Over time, the paralegal role has progressed with the technological changes taking place in the legal industry. The ABA's current definition of a paralegal is as follows:

A legal assistant or paralegal is a person, qualified by education, training or work experience who is employed or retained by a lawyer, law office, corporation, governmental agency or other entity and who performs specifically delegated substantive legal work for which a lawyer is responsible.

I know, I know. You read the definition of a paralegal and saw the term "legal assistant." Don't let this confuse you because the terms are used interchangeably in the legal industry, much like the terms attorney and lawyer. The use of each term depends upon the person and the region they live in. Most people are content being called legal assistants.

See, a paralegal and a legal assistant both perform substantive legal work. If that's the case, then why is the paralegal superior to the legal assistant in some law firms? Why do some attorneys treat legal assistants as if they are administrative assistants? This leads me to explain why I feel that the term legal assistant is confusing and misleading. Personally, I like the term paralegal. I'll explain why.

J'S TAKE ON PARALEGAL V. LEGAL ASSISTANT

There's already a misconception, with the general public, about who a legal assistant/paralegal is and what a legal assistant/paralegal does. Some of them think that the legal assistant/paralegal role can take the place of an attorney. Individuals try to get a paralegal to help them "draw up" documents and "fill out" forms (this is known as the unauthorized practice of law or UPL, which we will discuss later). They do this to try to save money. This is *no bueno*! While there are legal document preparers that can prepare legal documents for the general public, they cannot provide legal advice; they are not attorneys.

Okay. But what's wrong with the term legal assistant?

Those outside of the legal industry have been known to equate the term legal assistant with anyone who provides legal support or assistance to lawyers or law firms. In some minds, a legal assistant can be a legal administrative assistant, a receptionist, a file clerk, and the list goes on and on.

For someone who doesn't know the true meaning of paralegal and legal assistant, this person will automatically believe that a legal assistant is anyone who works in a law firm. This is wrong. Some kind of way, the term legal assistant has become the umbrella term for anyone (besides an attorney) who works in a law office or maybe even in the legal industry.

For this reason, I believe the term legal assistant can be complicating and misleading to those who are not informed of the differences between a legal assistant/paralegal and a legal administrative assistant. There are some attorneys who are uninformed and want their legal assistant to play the role of a legal administrative assistant, which is two separate roles.

A legal assistant can help with legal research, case analysis, argument and strategy. These two roles are rainmaking, profit generating roles when you use them the right way. A legal administrative assistant may assist with workflow, billing and filing documents with the court. I've learned that some attorneys want the legal assistant role to be broad when in fact it's not.

To minimize the confusion in my world about my role and what I do, I simply go by the term paralegal. I encourage you to take some time to talk to your support staff in these roles and see how they feel. Everyone and every region of the U.S. and the world has different thoughts towards the use of the terms. Just make sure you are using all support roles in the manner of which they were created to benefit you and your firm. Now that you are aware of the need of the paralegal profession and some of the chaos your firm may be experiencing, let's talk about the opportunity: how paralegals can help you and your firm.

❧ 3 ❧

KNOWING THE PARALEGAL
ROLE

"Go wherever the facts lead."

— SOCRATES

As MENTIONED BEFORE, THE PARALEGAL POSITION WAS created for a specific purpose. That purpose was to take a load off you (support) and to assist in providing greater access to legal services (reduce legal fees for clients). When you use the paralegal position outside of the intention it was created to be used, you have a problem. The problem is that you gamble with your time and money and undervalue the paralegal profession.

When utilized properly, paralegals can increase your bottom line through billing of their time. In *Missouri v. Jenkins*, 491 U.S. 274 (1989), the Supreme Court held that legal fees may include paralegal fees. Therefore, the proper use of paralegals can be a cost-effective way for you to deliver legal services to your customers.

When you use paralegals for legal tasks, it clears your schedule and allows you to maximize your time, thus generating profit for your firm. We all know that time is money. If your paralegal is not working on a billable task, your firm is losing money. You're hurting your bottom line.

This is the reason why you shouldn't use paralegals to make copies, to scan documents, and other administrative-related tasks. This is why your paralegal shouldn't run errands or type letters. Can they do these types of tasks? Of course they can. Do they want to do it and were they created for that? No. If these are the tasks you have your paralegal doing, you may need to reevaluate your firm's needs because at that point, they are not being a paralegal; they are being a secretary or an administrative assistant.

When you properly utilize your paralegal, the paralegal becomes an extension of you. A paralegal can do the exact same tasks you can do. The only difference is, a paralegal will not go before the court and argue a case, a paralegal will not represent your client, they won't set their own fees with your client and finally, the paralegal is not licensed to practice law or render a legal opinion. Those are the four distinct characteristics that separate a paralegal from a lawyer. We have to remind the general public that a paralegal is not a substitute for an attorney. The paralegal is a great asset to any law firm because this position is one that generates income for your firm.

TWO CATEGORIES OF PARALEGALS

This book's focus is the paralegal role in general. However, there are two categories of paralegals you may encounter throughout your career as an attorney. There's the traditional, in-house paralegal and the contract paralegal, also known as freelance/contract/virtual. Both provide great benefits for your law practice, they just operate in different ways.

The traditional, in-house paralegal will work alongside you, face to face in an office or in a brick and mortar location. You will be able to walk up to this person's office or desk or even yell across the room to communicate with them, if it suits you. A traditional, in-house paralegal may be a full-time or part-time employee where you will more than likely pay for their benefits, time off, provide them with office equipment, a space to work, and the tools they need to do the work. You are also responsible for their employment taxes, workers' compensation insurance and other responsibilities that come with hiring employees. Sometimes, you may need to train the traditional, in-house paralegal on certain tasks and how you like things done, and you will control their work hours and when they take lunch and breaks.

The contract/freelance/virtual paralegal takes on two separate characteristics of its own. A contract/freelance paralegal can work literally alongside you or remotely alongside you. When a paralegal works remotely, they are known as virtual paralegals.

Oftentimes, this category of paralegal operates as a business, thereby providing a service. The contract/freelance paralegal may choose to work in-house under contract with agreed-upon terms and conditions or remotely, under contract with agreed-upon terms and conditions. They usually work with several attorneys at once, much like you work with many clients at once.

You will sign an agreement to work with them and you will pay them according to their payment structure. For your law firm, they may serve as a vendor, as they are providing a service. Because they are a vendor or a contractor, they are not employed by your firm. You have no control over the hours they work nor do you control how they do the work. They come to you ready to go with their own equipment and tools for getting the job done. For the paralegals who have ventured into this line of work, they are experts of their craft and are professionals.

For this reason, you wouldn't need to provide any type of training. An added benefit of working with this kind of paralegal is that they are responsible for their own taxes, workspace, equipment, office, etc. This is where you save money, can make a profit and can provide a service to your clients at a reduced cost, keeping them happy and returning to you for legal services. Now that we know why paralegals were created, what they can and can't do, let's turn our attention to where paralegals are needed.

OH, THE PLACES A PARALEGAL CAN GO

The paralegal role is not tied directly to a law firm. An attorney is not directly tied to a law firm either. Much like attorneys, paralegals are needed in almost every industry simply because the law touches every aspect of society.

You may find paralegals working at government agencies, within the non-profit sector, corporate legal departments, and any other private or public organization. Paralegals are equipped with a wide range of skills and talents, such as the ability to hunt for information, keep the legal team abreast of the case status, analyze mass amounts of records and organize documents. Paralegals are also great writers and have a way with words to persuade a judge in a motion. Paralegals are usually on the front line of client contact. They serve as a point guard for you. While you're in court and meeting with new clients, the paralegal will sometimes be your client's first lifeline by keeping your clients in the know. Paralegals may also help you strategize your next plan of attack in a case and keep you on track.

To say that a paralegal's skillset is only needed in law firms would be an inaccurate. Paralegals are needed in insurance companies, real estate agencies, non-profits, the military, corporations, at the public defender's office, and medical companies.

Be mindful of how you treat your paralegals because they have many options when it comes to the places they can go. If you are an attorney who does not understand the paralegal role and ends up underutilizing the paralegal, he or she will become bored and may leave for one of the above-mentioned places or create his/her own company because they know the value they bring to the table.

❦ 4 ❦

ATTORNEY + PARALEGAL = PROFIT

USE PARALEGALS THE RIGHT WAY AND STOP LEAVING MONEY ON THE TABLE

"Growth and profit are a product of how people work together."

— RICARDO SEMLER

AFTER SPEAKING WITH SEVERAL SOLO ATTORNEYS ABOUT their legal support needs for their law practice, I realized that the way they are operating their law practice was wrong on many different levels. The primary issue lay within their approach to being a solo attorney.

They believe they must do everything alone and that they will not be able to find anyone to help them. They like the sound of the benefits a paralegal or a legal support service provider can bring to the table and immediately begin to imagine a life where they can delegate legal tasks to either a paralegal or service provider and in a jiffy, as Olivia Pope says, "It's handled." They start to envision a world where their lives are easier and less stressful because of the help they could have. Then, they immediately jump off cloud 9 when they hear the standard rates of the paralegal or service provider and go into the "I can't afford this" mode. Why? Because they haven't taken the time to incorporate a paralegal rate into their firm's standard rate practices. Let's get you on the path to profit, shall we?

The paralegal position was created to benefit you and your firm. When your paralegal performs substantive legal tasks, these are billable items on your firm's invoice to the client. Remember, paralegal fees may be included as legal fees, as was the case with *Missouri v. Jenkins*, 491 U.S. 274 (1989). The more work your paralegal does, the less your client pays for legal services. This is how paralegals expand the reach of legal services in the community, and this is how we help you to generate profit for your firm. Most importantly, we keep your clients happy and they keep coming back to you for services. See the cycle here? While we're working on those legal tasks, you could be focused on bringing in new clients, thus increasing your streams of revenue. If you're tied down to the day-to-day operations of your law practice, you leave money on the table.

HOW TO ESTABLISH PARALEGAL RATES WITHIN YOUR FIRM

Let's say your hourly rate as an attorney is $300 an hour. You voice this to your clients during the initial client meeting and have this rate listed in your fee agreements so your clients are well informed. Within your fee agreement, you also state that a paralegal may work on the case, but for some reason, you don't specify a paralegal rate.

As a result, your paralegal performs some of the work on the case and at the end of the month, you send an invoice to your client solely for the work you've done on the case, at the $300 an hour rate. This is wrong because you don't make a profit this way. As a matter of fact, you're defeating the purpose of paralegals: to expand the reach of legal services and reduce legal fees for clients. Your paralegal rate should be at least half of your rate, making the paralegal rate $150 an hour. You can reap the benefits of generating revenue even while you're not working or working on an entirely different case.

Let's say you eventually you decide to retain a virtual paralegal support provider to outsource some of your paralegal tasks to minimize overwhelming your in-house paralegal. That service provider will have her own billing rate for her attorney clients. Now, when a virtual paralegal works on your case, your firm bills your client $150 an hour (your firm's standard paralegal rate) for the work the paralegal has performed.

When you receive an invoice from your virtual paralegal support provider, using her own billing rate, this rate should be significantly lower than your firm's standard paralegal rate. Check out the profit margin that lies between your rates and your virtual paralegal support service provider rate.

Category	Hourly Rate
Attorney	$300
Paralegal	$150
Paralegal Support Service Provider	$75

Just keep in mind that a virtual paralegal support service provider is a business and/or independent contractor. This means you don't pay employee taxes or have the need to create additional space in your office to accommodate the provider. And don't forget, the amount you pay your virtual paralegal support service provider is also a tax-deductible expense. Can you say, money in the bank?

Here you can see how a paralegal minimizes your client's legal fees, generates profit for your firm, saves you time and makes your life easier. There's no reason as to why you can't afford a paralegal. Stop undervaluing your legal services and gambling with your time and money. You can't afford not to incorporate a paralegal in your firm.

THE PARALEGAL IS NOT A CATCH-ALL POSITION IN A LAW FIRM

I've witnessed many instances where law firms or even solo attorneys have a well-trained, educated and qualified paralegal, but they use the paralegal as a catch-all position, wearing several hats and playing several roles all at once. The paralegal is not a catch-all position. Allow me to explain why this is wrong and why it is also considered the under-utilization of the capacity in which the paralegal was created.

According to an article I recently read titled, "Lawyers are from Mars and Paralegals are from Venus" by Cheryl J. Leone of Atkinson-Baker, "The use of non-lawyer professionally skilled paralegals is still in its infancy. Lawyers still do not know how to use paralegals and some are threatened that a non-lawyer can be used at such a high level. They want a worker bee when, in fact, they have a thinking bee." When lawyers are in law school, they are not taught how the paralegal position has a positive impact on a firm. When they come out of school and begin work, they have no clue as to the skills and talents that paralegals possess, so they automatically think that it is okay to use a paralegal for any and all administrative type tasks that need to be completed.

Paralegals were created for substantive legal tasks: What attorneys don't understand is that some paralegals have taken the time to hone their craft and have voluntarily educated themselves to be able to perform substantive legal tasks, just like an attorney (but under attorney supervision of course). Remember the American Bar Association's definition of a paralegal?

A legal assistant or paralegal is a person, qualified by education, training or work experience who is employed or retained by a lawyer, law office, corporation, governmental agency or other entity and who performs specifically delegated substantive legal work for which a lawyer is responsible.

Attorneys Fail in Their Pursuit to Save Money: So, if a paralegal can perform the same tasks as an attorney, why would an attorney want to use a paralegal to be a secretary, a bookkeeper, an office manager, a runner, a file clerk and a receptionist? It's simple: to try to save money. But this is where they have it all wrong. In the long-run, they are left with an overwhelmed and overworked paralegal who just wants to write motions and briefs, analyze documents and perform research. Instead the paralegal is busy creating invoices, filing documents, answering phones, cleaning the office, etc.

Because the paralegal is not being used in the proper capacity to perform substantive legal tasks, the paralegal leaves the firm to find work that is complimentary to his or her skill set, qualifications, and education. The attorney lost the paralegal, probably a valuable one, and must start over to find a new one. I don't know about you, but I think good paralegals are hard to come by. This takes more time from the attorney, which could have been used as billable hours towards a case, but now that time must be logged under admin time, aka nonbillable. This results in the firm losing money overall.

The Solution to It All: Attorneys must be diligent in their use of paralegals and their legal staff. Your best solution is to thoroughly evaluate the positions in your office, determine what your needs are and use the positions for the reasons they were created.

What do I mean? Well, let your receptionist answer the phone and handle incoming guests at the office. Allow your secretary to type up your letters. Let your file clerk organize your files and let your runner run the errands in the office, not your office manager. Let your paralegal perform research, analysis and legal writing. When you work in your power, practicing law, you give your support staff the opportunity to work in theirs, supporting you.

PARALEGAL DOS AND DON'TS

The definition of a paralegal is still pretty hazy. I get it. The definition is broad. Just think of it this way: a paralegal can perform the same tasks that you can, under your supervision. When you think about the various tasks that you do on any given day, you'll have a better understanding as to what paralegals can help you with.

Generally speaking, a paralegal's role is to support the attorney. On the other hand, there are some tasks that a paralegal is not allowed to perform. Those tasks are associated with the unauthorized practice of law (UPL). This is one of the major differences between an attorney and a paralegal. Let's observe some of the things that a paralegal cannot do:

- Render a legal opinion or give legal advice
- Set legal fees
- Represent clients in court

This is a small list. Generally, a paralegal can assist with any other tasks ranging from initial client intake to discovery to trial. The difference is, you *can* practice law. You have the license to provide legal services. A paralegal cannot provide legal services.

5

FLYING FIRST-CLASS WITH
COACH MINDSETS

"Quality is remembered long after the price is forgotten."

— SIR HENRY ROYCE

ONE OF MY BEST FRIENDS AND I LOVE TO TALK ABOUT THE days of working in a law firm together. At the time, I was a legal assistant and she was the law firm administrator. I like to think of her as my astro twin. We're both Taurus women, with birthdays 6 days apart and very similar personalities. We learned some valuable lessons that we use in our careers today. Many of those lessons gave me the big picture on law firm logistics.

Whenever we talk about the legal industry and how fixed peoples' minds are when it comes to practicing law, hiring people and the overall operations of a law firm, I always use this analogy:

You can't fly first-class with a coach mindset.

The first time I said this phrase, we both laughed but afterwards, we realized how true it is. I know some of you may feel like I'm taking a hit at you, but everything starts with your mind. Either you will accept it and grow from it or you will be upset and stay in the position you're in right now and get left behind. Allow me to explain some of the fixated mentalities we often find ourselves in.

On a day-to-day basis, I see attorneys and law firms placing ads on hiring platforms such as Indeed, Zip Recruiter and the like to hire people like paralegals to provide support to their firm. A month or two goes by, and I see those same attorneys looking for help. Eventually, they take these ads to social media. Why? Because they say they've been getting horrible resumes on whatever hiring platform they've been using, be it Indeed, Zip Recruiter or Craigslist. The post on Facebook looks something like this:

I need help! I pay. I need a paralegal with experience.
My law firm is growing and we are in need of paralegal help. If you
know of anyone looking for a paralegal position, please have them
send their resume to info@abclawfirm.com.

Need a new paralegal. Will train. Call 555-5555 or email resume to
me@lawfirm.com.

And sometimes these ads are found on LinkedIn because it's a professional networking site. Surely, a qualified person can be found there, right? All of a sudden, they start to get responses from paralegals on Facebook and/or LinkedIn, and this is where these attorneys reveal their true state of mind.

The paralegal says, "Sure, what do you need help with?" or, "How can I help?"

The attorney asks, "Are you in my area?" The paralegal responds, "No, I'm not in your area but based on your ad, I am qualified to do the work." The attorney responds, "Well I prefer someone in my area who is familiar with our local rules here." See, this is a problem. The attorney is in a fixed mindset and can't see past the fact that most times, the greatest paralegals are not in the same local area. If this sounds familiar, you'll miss the mark when looking for qualified people to do the work because you're hung up on your personal want to have someone in your local area. You miss out on valuable, first-class people who can provide great service to you. Instead, you settle for people in your local area, and despite the horrible resumes you complained about, you end up hiring someone and then you are stuck with having to train them.

As a result, you've spent countless hours preparing an ad, reviewing resumes, and interviewing candidates. Those hours could have been well spent on your clients' cases. In the end, you're still unhappy. You eventually look to outsource some tasks but once you find out the costs to have those tasks outsourced, you wonder why the fees are significantly higher than paralegals in your area. Or, you wonder why you should even retain the services of a paralegal when you can get a contracted attorney. You have such high standards for yourself, your practice and the quality of work you provide your clients (first-class mentality), but you want to get high-quality performance for less (coach mentality).

Because you have this coach mentality, it's difficult for you to fly first-class. First-class knocked on your door and you didn't care to open it, due to your coach mentality. Instead, you settled for the paralegal in your area, who may not be as qualified to get the job done. You spend time coaching, training and holding this person's hand. Meanwhile, you're leaving money on the table because you can't see the true value of the paralegal you've hired because you're misusing him anyway by using him for administrative-type tasks, making him the office manager and all sorts of nonsense that has nothing to do with the role of a paralegal.

YOU CAN'T SEE THE TRUE VALUE OF PARALEGALS IF YOU ARE MISUSING THEM.

A paralegal is a first-class resource, if you know how to use them properly. Because most attorneys don't value paralegals the way they should, and some paralegals don't own up to their own value, we are in a constant battle. Think about how you feel when you fly first-class.

- You fly in front, which means you get on and off the plane first.
- You have the best seats. They are comfortable and spacious with plenty of leg room.
- Better service. You get direct attention from your flight attendant.
- It's quiet. The environment is not as noisy and you have less people around.

When you fly first-class, you make an investment in yourself, your comfort, and your environment. Hiring a paralegal is an investment in your law practice. And just like first-class, a paralegal will and should cost more than your coach mindset. Look at it this way: What is your time, your convenience and your peace of mind worth?

❧ 6 ❧

LETTING GO OF THE TRADITIONAL WAYS OF THE LEGAL INDUSTRY

"Change is the law of life and if you look to the past, you'll miss the future."

— JOHN F. KENNEDY

EXPLORING THE WORLD OF VIRTUAL PARALEGALS

I'VE BEEN IN THE WORKING WORLD LONG ENOUGH TO know that unless someone works in certain types of industries, like production, manufacturing, and trucking, you don't work a full 8 hours a day. It is my belief that no one truly works an 8-hour day outside of those certain industries I described. Today, I want you to open your mind a bit to see where I'm headed with this. Do you have any idea where your money is going? When you pay your full-time employees, if you have any, are you paying them for their presence in the office or are you paying them for performance, meaning the work that they do? If you've never thought about this, let's move forward.

PRESENCE V. PERFORMANCE

In 2012, I had the opportunity to work for a solo attorney, and it was probably the best work situation for me as an employee. But now that I'm a business owner, I've realized that solo attorneys and maybe some small law firms shell out so much money on presence when performance happens on occasion.

Sometimes your workload does not allow for you to have a full-time, 8-hour employee. But because this is the way you are accustomed to operating, you end up spending tons of money on presence when you really need performance. You feel like you need to have a "face in the place" in order to get things done. Still not tracking? Allow me to explain.

Employee A is your full-time employee, and although they are always there when you need them, they spend most of the time sitting at the desk, checking Facebook, Twitter, and other forms of social media. They also email their friends and family and may even send a few texts throughout the day. They do this because there are no tasks which I call "hot" and nothing is pressing right at the moment. Sure, they've sent over discovery requests, but they have to wait a month to get the responses back, right?

Let's say you've converted to electronic filing, so there's not much paperwork to be physically filed. Oh, and let's not talk about billing because that's only done once a month. Furthermore, no one enters your office without an appointment. Sure, you may get phone calls here or there but most people contact you via email anyway. Are you with me now?

What I'm saying is that you may need to re-evaluate your office structure. Stop wasting time and money paying for someone's presence in the office when you don't have 8 hours' worth of work for an employee to do.

Consider the many options that are available to you today. You don't have to work like the attorneys on *Matlock* and *Perry Mason*. And let's not forget that Perry Mason had a paralegal. Bonus points to you if you can remember her name and let me know on LinkedIn. But, have you thought about telecommuting, working remotely or even outsourcing some of your work? Doing so can save you money on benefits. When you outsource your work to a contract/virtual paralegal, you save! Not only that, you get the performance you pay for when you need it.

WORKING WITH VIRTUAL PARALEGALS IS ALL ABOUT YOUR FRAME OF MIND

Virtual paralegals are known as contract, independent or freelance paralegals who may be business owners running paralegal and legal support companies hired by attorneys, law firms, corporate legal departments and legal programs to provide support services through the use of remote access systems. While the notion of enlisting the help of a paralegal who may be hundreds of miles away sounds absurd, because (1) you can't see them, and (2) you can't monitor their progress on tasks, doesn't mean you cannot get adequate legal support. Getting the help from and working with a virtual paralegal is all about your frame of mind.

The question is not what the paralegal can do for you. The question is whether your personality will allow you to obtain the services of a virtual paralegal. The answer to this question lies within you. The answer requires a thorough self-examination of yourself.

You must look deep within and study your own behavior, thoughts, and emotions that are a part of your genetic makeup. Take some time to observe your strengths and weaknesses. Take a step back and see how you manage your time, your tasks and your law practice. Here, you will be able to determine whether your personality will allow you to retain the services of a virtual paralegal.

After your self-examination, if you find that your personality is any of the following, a virtual paralegal may not be a fit for you and your firm's culture:

Micromanager: A well-trained paralegal does not need to be told how to do their job.

Procrastinator: Paralegals don't avoid tasks. The sooner you inform your paralegal of a task, the better.

Vague Communicator: Clear, specific and organized communication is key in working with a paralegal.

With that being said, all attorneys are not the same. The same can be said about paralegals. The take-away from this message is to find a paralegal who complements your personality.

While this may be a match made in heaven, there may be some attorneys who have these qualities that need that push from a paralegal. If you find a paralegal who can do that for you, that's great! However, that push may not come from a virtual paralegal. An in-house paralegal may be better suited for your needs.

I HIRED A VIRTUAL PARALEGAL – NOW WHAT?

Well, congratulations! You've hired a virtual paralegal, which means you've crossed over to the new realm of legal support and paralegalism filled with technology and the ability to get work done without having to look a person in the face. This tells me that you're not afraid to take risks. Sure, hiring a virtual paralegal is a risk. Being a virtual paralegal is a risk. But you have to take the risk to get the reward, right?

So now that you've hired your virtual paralegal, you may be wondering what to do next. You've never done this before and you have no clue what to do. The first thing you need to know about hiring a virtual paralegal is that it is more than a contractor relationship. When you hire a virtual paralegal, yes, you're hiring a contractor, but you're hiring a partner. You've hired someone who will treat your work as if they are sitting in the office with you. They will treat the cases as if they are their own. Why? Because virtual paralegals are business owners too. They have standards to follow, just like you. Ethics anyone?

What's next for you is ultimately decided between you and your virtual paralegal. The virtual paralegal can be as involved in your cases and daily routine as you like. Your virtual paralegal can perform research for you and write briefs when you simply don't have the time. The virtual paralegal may even make client contact for you, organize your electronic files, schedule events on your calendar and more! The possibilities here are endless.

If you feel like you need to "see" your virtual paralegal, you can conduct a video chat session to plan out your week, map out the strategies on your cases and discuss your plans for the future. Just be careful. If you've hired someone as a virtual paralegal and you've only tasked them with administrative-type tasks, such as invoicing, answering the phone, drafting letters, uploading documents to your electronic files and ordering your supplies, you didn't need a virtual paralegal. What you needed was a legal secretary. It's okay because mistakes will be made and learned from. Just be honest with yourself and your firm's needs and find the best possible solution that will help you reach your goals.

IS A VIRTUAL LEGAL SUPPORT TEAM RIGHT FOR YOU?

Solo attorneys who run paperless and virtual law firms have many options when it comes to getting a helping hand with the operations of their business. One of those options is to hire an employee. The other option is to retain a contractor in a physical or virtual capacity. This contractor can come in many forms and may be presented as an employee of a temp agency, a freelancer or a company specializing in a solo attorney's needs. This contractor you seek may be someone who would work in-house (meaning your office) or someone who would work remotely or virtually (meaning their office or some other remote location). This can make for a tough decision, but I'm here to help.

HOW TO DECIDE IF VIRTUAL LEGAL SUPPORT IS RIGHT FOR YOU.

This is a simple process if you take the time to do it right. Let's take it step by step and review what I call the 4Cs of the deciding factors for virtual legal support:

Clientele. Take a look at your client base. Are they baby boomers? Generation Y? Do they make contact with your office through email or snail mail? Do they pick up the phone to call you about any and everything? When you ask them to send a document to your office, will they scan and send through email or do they use a postage stamp and make you wait a day to receive it? If the majority of your clients don't mind visiting with you through a video conference software system such as Skype or Zoom, a virtual legal support team may be the right fit for you.

Clock. Review your time-tracking software for last month. See how much time you spent on billable hours verses non-billable hours. If your non-billable hours outweigh your billable hours, you need to bring in a virtual legal support team to lend a helping hand. If you are not tracking your non-billable hours, or as some like to call it, admin hours, try this for one week and see where your time is spent. This will give you a good idea of how much time you are spending on tasks that do not generate income. You have to stop gambling with your time and leaving money on the table.

Communication and Collaboration. Check yourself and observe how you work with others. Do you clearly communicate or do others have to constantly ask you to repeat yourself because they don't understand what you need? Are you able to collaborate virtually using email, instant messaging and project management software? Do you maintain clean and concise electronic files or is it hard for you to find the last document you uploaded? If you cannot properly communicate and collaborate, don't give yourself a headache trying to work with anyone virtually or remotely. Save yourself some headaches and get in-house support instead.

3 THINGS YOU SHOULD KNOW ABOUT VIRTUAL PARALEGALS

If you've read any of my articles, you know my message by now: paralegals must be utilized properly and virtual paralegals should be used as a firm resource in the same capacity. Someone reading this article may be thinking, "Paralegals sound good but I just don't have enough work to hire a full-time paralegal, nor can I afford to hire one right now."

You know what I say to your line of thinking? I say, "Great!" Based on your way of thinking, you may be able to benefit from retaining support from a virtual paralegal. That's if you're ready to do something different, of course. Before you take that leap of faith, there are 3 things you should know about virtual paralegals.

Virtual Paralegals Are a Great Alternative to Hiring a Full-Time Paralegal. You said you didn't think you could hire a full-time paralegal? No worries! A virtual paralegal is an awesome way to get the support you need when you need it the most! You don't have to worry about handling those mundane tasks (that lawyers shouldn't do anyway); you don't have to worry about being in court when your mind is clearly somewhere else writing a brief or doing research; and most importantly, a virtual paralegal can free time for you to focus on other pressing matters or even marketing.

A recent article I read from *Find Law* noted a Thompson Reuters report showing that attorneys practicing in boutique firms only spend 17 percent of their time on marketing and managing their firm.

You already know that paralegals can do the same tasks you can do, it's just a matter of you being willing to delegate those tasks. Virtual paralegals can handle the majority of the tasks a traditional in-house paralegal would, such as writing briefs, performing legal research and investigation, due diligence, scheduling depositions, client intake, managing electronic files, drafting discovery tools, requesting medical records, etc.

Virtual Paralegals Are Business Owners, Not Employees. Too many times I have seen attorney and law firm ads online asking for a virtual paralegal's help all while seeking to micromanage. One ad read, "More independence will be given over time." Hello...when you retain the services of a virtual paralegal, you need to understand that this person is an independent contractor, not an employee. The majority of virtual paralegals run their own businesses.

If you're an attorney that is looking to hover, micromanage and dictate how and when tasks are to be performed, your best option is to hire an employee. If you do hire a virtual paralegal and you are controlling that person's schedule, providing them with necessary tools that they should have to complete the tasks at hand, you may have an employee and not an independent contractor. Be careful because the IRS is cracking down on the distinction between an employee and an independent contractor.

Virtual Paralegals Can Be Applied to Any Area of the Law. No matter the specialty, virtual paralegals can be beneficial to you. It's even better when you can locate a virtual paralegal who specializes in the same area of law. Just like traditional paralegals, virtual paralegals come with their own specialties and preferences in the areas of law in which they choose to work. Don't miss out on your opportunity to get the support you need when you need it.

A NEW ERA OF WORKING WITH PARALEGALS

Solo attorneys cannot always afford to hire in-house staff. As a matter of fact, sometimes the work of a small law firm does not expend a full 8-hour day. What happens is the attorneys and small law firms end up paying someone to sit in the office. That person becomes bored with no work to do and can spend countless hours on social media or other non-work-related tasks just to make their day go by. I call this paying for presence rather than performance. Attorneys end up paying to have a face in the place even when there is no productivity or performance being made.

When an attorney decides to utilize our services, that attorney will only pay for the performance of the work. Since the legal industry is slowly embracing technology with e-filing, cloud-based case management and online legal research, this is a win-win for attorneys and legal support professionals. This performance verses presence concept also applies to other industries. Employers should be diligent in deciding whether utilizing an in-house staff member verses a virtual staff member is best for their company.

BENEFITS OF WORKING VIRTUALLY

For businesses considering whether to introduce the concept of virtual work (also called working remotely or telecommuting) to their employees or contractors, there are several benefits:

- It's affordable
- You have happier and healthier workers
- Working virtually is eco-friendly
- You and your team will have increased productivity

Working virtually is not for everyone. Take time to decide if it is best for you and your business. You don't want to hinder your business because you didn't give it a chance. Also, change is inevitable. With statistics from the American Community Survey showing that 3.7 million people work from home, we can see that working virtually is the future of work, and it's here to stay.

THE ONE THING SOME ATTORNEYS DO WRONG

Let's talk about support for a while. Support is one of those aspects of a law firm that you, attorneys and law firms, need in order to survive. Some say they can't make it without the support of their secretary or assistant or paralegal. Others even say they are only as good as their support staff. While these are all true statements, when some of you are in a bind and need help, you miss out on the opportunity to get the support you need most: the support from contract and virtual paralegals.

I recently had a conversation with an attorney who needed help, like yesterday. She just got to this law firm and has over 200 cases in the areas of medical malpractice, personal injury and insurance defense, which are the areas I absolutely love! She talked to me about how she hadn't been able to find qualified help. She mentioned that she did not have time to train anyone. She said she was very impressed with my bio and litigation support consultant profile. However, she broke the news and said she wanted a full-time employee.

I cringed. I asked her a few questions and gave her my spiel about all the value I could offer her as a contract paralegal. The firm would save money, wouldn't have to pay benefits, they would reduce their bottom line and make their clients happier with a lower bill each month, and most importantly, she would obtain the assistance of a top-notch paralegal who is well-developed and ready to go! I was the solution to a problem, and because this attorney was in a traditional state of mind, she was on the fence about my offer and wanted to mull things over.

GOOD HELP IS HARD TO FIND...

We all know that good help is hard to find. It truly is hard to find. But when you've found it, you should jump on the opportunity to take it. It doesn't come around that often. Don't miss out on the chance to have good help when you need it. Who's to say that you need to have an employee? As long as the work gets done, why not outsource the work, save money and hire a contract paralegal?

...BUT NOT WHEN YOU CONSIDER THE MANY POSSIBILITIES

We live in a different age. Legal work can get done efficiently and accurately whether someone is in-house physically or is remote over the internet. It is not hard to work with a paralegal who is already familiar with your chosen specialty of the law to pick up the work and run with it to make your job easier.

You, the attorney, have to be open-minded and consider all possibilities these days, because your best candidate to help you meet your need may not be an employee. Your best candidate may just be a company like Pinnacle Litigation Connections, LLC, and simply because you refuse to open your eyes to a different way of running your law practice, you miss out on some of the best-of-the-best paralegals you will ever meet.

❧ 7 ❧

THE GOODNESS OF VIRTUAL PARALEGALS

"Goodness is the only investment that never fails."

— HENRY DAVID THOREAU

AS THE LEGAL INDUSTRY CONTINUES TO GROW AND embrace technology, so do the paralegals. In your firm, paralegals are what keep things going. They are the glue to holding the firm together. What happens when your paralegal is out for a considerable amount of time due to maternity leave or vacation? Your first thought is to hire an employment agency to find a temporary employee. That's a great idea, but it is not the best idea. The best solution is to think outside the box and hire a contract and virtual paralegal. Here are 3 simple reasons why contract and virtual paralegals are good for your firm:

1. Contract and virtual paralegals won't break the bank.

Law firms and solo attorneys can actually save money by

hiring contract and virtual paralegals. We won't break the bank because we don't need office space and you don't pay employee taxes or other employment-related benefits. You only pay for the services you need, rather than paying an employee to sit in the office and be on Facebook or Twitter for part of the day after completing tasks.

2. Contract and virtual paralegals are wizards with technology.

Contract and virtual paralegals are technology mavens. We have to be hip to the latest technology because our job depends on it considering the use of PACER, ECF filings, E-Discovery, OCR, and case management tools. Contract and virtual paralegals are ones to attend technology trade shows, CLEs and seminars to stay informed about the latest and greatest technology that will save money, time, maximize efficiency, and increase productivity. I just attended a CLE that covered the ABA updates regarding competence when it comes to technology and how ethics requires attorneys to also be informed about the benefits and risks associated with the use of technology.

3. Contract and virtual paralegals are self-sufficient. No training involved.

Contract and virtual paralegals can be assigned any task and will see it through to completion. If you hire a contract and virtual paralegal, you must be able to trust them. Trust and understand that we have specialized skills, training, experience, and education in providing you with the support you need. Sometimes, this doesn't work out so well, leaving attorneys rejecting the new era of legal support: virtual paralegals.

THE NUMBER 1 REASON WHY ATTORNEYS REJECT VIRTUAL PARALEGALS – DON'T LET THIS BE YOU...

No matter what type of law they specialize in, at some point, all virtual paralegals experience a time where they are rejected by you. The problem is, virtual paralegals can't seem to figure out why they are being rejected. They've built an amazing service-based business to serve you, they've done impeccable work for their attorney clients, they have a laundry list of references and they still hear excuses as to why attorneys like you don't want to work with them. Those excuses sound something like this:

- I can't afford a virtual paralegal.
- Oh, you're not in my area? I want someone in my area familiar with our rules.
- Why should I hire a virtual paralegal when I can hire an attorney on Hire an Esquire?
- I think outsourcing tasks to you would make things harder for me.
- This will make my staff work more.

Any of these sound familiar? Have you used one of these excuses before? For some reason, when a virtual paralegal extends their hand to help you (because you've clearly stated, "I need help," or you've posted, "Anyone know a good paralegal?" on social media), you hem and haw and come up with all sorts of excuses as to why you don't want their help. So you sit there, alone, and continue to waste time and money with your paralegal search.

I know these excuses exist, because I've been there too. I'm also standing alongside virtual paralegals who've heard similar rejections. Now truth be told, some of you reject virtual paralegals because you're simply not equipped to see their true value. Quite frankly, if you can't see the value of a paralegal, you definitely won't see the value of a virtual paralegal. But I'll save that topic for a different article. Let me get to the heart of this discussion:

The #1 reason why attorneys reject virtual paralegals is TRUST.

Trust is an interesting thing, isn't it? Trust is a major component of relationships. Without trust, you have no relationship. When an attorney retains (not hires) the services of a virtual paralegal, that attorney is gaining a partner and a relationship is formed. You, my friend, can't get to this point of forming relationships and partnerships if you don't have the ability to trust.

"If you don't have trust inside your company, you can't transfer it to your customers."

— ROGER STAUBACH

It's funny to me how you expect your clients and potential clients to trust you with their legal issues, sensitive information and stories they will more than likely tell no one else. How can you expect for someone to trust you if you can't give trust to anyone? You know, trust is much like energy. Energy can be transferred. It can be given and it can be taken away. The same goes for trust. Trust can be transferred; it can be given and it can be taken away. Don't expect someone to give you something when you are unable to give it.

THE WORK OF THE LEGAL INDUSTRY IS BIGGER THAN YOU

In order to establish trust, it will take some work on your part to get to the root cause of the issue. Maybe something happened to where you're uncomfortable with trust. But what I need for you to understand is that this work that we do as legal professionals is bigger than you. It's bigger than me. Take some time to think about the reason why you became an attorney. What is your why? What is your mission? What is your purpose? If you can't answer this, you have a real problem.

I say the work of the legal industry is bigger than you because sometimes you forget about the big picture. The big picture of the legal industry is to provide legal services and make those services accessible for everyone. Now, if you're letting your trust issues keep you from providing legal services and keeping costs down for your clients, you're hindering the work of the legal industry. Don't let your personal issues with trust make you lose sight of the reason why we are here.

Dear attorneys, help me to help you. If you contact me or any other virtual/remote/contract paralegal, be ready to be open-minded. Do not shut us out because we run our own businesses and don't want to be employees. Come on, solo attorneys; you know the feeling. You remember starting your own practice and you never looked back. Same goes for us. Don't expect for us to shut down our business to be your employee. In order to support you, you have to support us. We created our businesses to be able to reach out and help attorneys and law firms wherever they are and whenever they need it so that everyone can get the quality help they deserve. The solution to your legal support woes may be right in front of your eyes on your computer or phone screen. All you have to do is pick up the phone, send a message, or an email. Are you next?

GRATITUDE

I appreciate you for investing in *Strike That* and entrusting me to shed light on the paralegal profession. Because of you, the work lives of many paralegals will be better simply because you took time to understand the impact the paralegal has on the legal industry.

It is my hope that this book serves as an eye opener for attorneys and paralegals and leads to a harmonious relationship between the two. I challenge you to take the knowledge you've just gained throughout this book and develop key, actionable steps to apply to your law practice. I look forward to hearing how *Strike That* helped you re-evaluate the paralegal role in your firm.

J Bazier

ABOUT THE AUTHOR

Jaquetta "J" Bazier is the visionary force behind Pinnacle Litigation Connections LLC. She's always had an eagle eye for the law and knew she wanted to work in the legal field at a very early age. J began her career as a legal professional in her early 20s in Oklahoma City, OK, after working in the claims department for a Fortune 500 insurance company.

Throughout her legal tenure, she has absorbed and experienced every aspect of law firm operations and held positions such as file clerk, runner receptionist, legal secretary, office manager, and paralegal at large and small firms alike. She's even trained new support staff and newly-minted attorneys on legal procedures, techniques and the ins and outs of a law firm. These experiences have led her to gain insight on how law firms can improve in matters such as communication, law practice management, and strategy through the use of paralegals.

As a paralegal who has quickly built a successful career path specializing in civil litigation and document management, J has supported attorneys throughout every aspect of their law practice. Now, as the founder of a virtual legal support company, she aims to support modern day solo attorneys and small firms whenever the need it, no matter their location. Her intelligence, combined with an aggressive spirit and no-nonsense persona, results in fast, accurate, and effective litigation support for any lawyer. Her legal experience includes work in insurance defense, medical malpractice, workers' compensation, personal injury, oil and gas law, employment law, products liability and real estate law.

As a military spouse, she has worked for government contractors and some of the top law firms in Oklahoma City and for a trial lawyer in Tulsa, Oklahoma, and she quickly drew recognition in the State of Kansas. Her essay, "No Courts, No Justice, No Freedom," was featured in the Central Oklahoma Association of Legal Assistants (COALA) newsletter (L.A. Times, Volume 31 Number 1) for the State of Oklahoma's Law Day celebration, and she was highly recommended to become a paralegal and trial/litigation preparer for the U.S. Attorney's Office in Topeka, Kansas. J attended the Legal Assistant Education Program at the University of Oklahoma's College of Law and received a Paralegal Certificate from Kansas State University in conjunction with the Center for Legal Studies. A

Montgomery, Alabama, native, she attended Tuskegee University and majored in political science.

Outside of the office, J can be found advocating for kids in foster care as a Court Appointed Special Advocate (CASA), answering the call for civil rights as a member of the NAACP, reading, working on her authorship journey, and being a listening ear or voice of reason for those near and dear to her. She enjoys helping others, spending time with family, soaking up the sun by taking a run or walk at the nearest park, visiting wineries and shoe shopping.

Connect with J
www.linkedin.com/in/jbazier

THE SHIFT EFFECT

Learn about J's growth mindset program, The Shift Effect.

Shift your perception
Shift your performance
Shift your profits

The Shift Effect or simply "Shift" is a 3-step results-oriented growth mindset program, created by a litigation paralegal, designed to help solo attorneys eliminate their objections, hesitancies and fears about the new era of legal support: virtual paralegals.

Shift is for the solo attorney who, for some reason, let the legal industry and its old-school ways affect how they practice law and how they run their law practice. If you're an attorney who loves new ideas and fresh concepts but needs to get unstuck, Shift is the program for you.

Find out more at:
www.theshifteffect.pinnaclelitigationconnections.com

PINNACLE LITIGATION CONNECTIONS

THE ATTORNEY'S BEST FRIEND IN CIVIL LITIGATION

Pinnacle Litigation Connections is a legal support company providing virtual litigation support solutions for the non-traditional, modern day attorney and law firm.

For information on virtual legal support solutions for your law firm or corporate legal department, visit:

www.pinnaclelitigationconnections.com

Join the Attorney's Best Friend Club

www.bit.ly/attorneysbestfriendclub

See Pinnacle Litigation Connections featured in:

www.practicepanther.com/law-firm-week-pinnacle-litigation-connections-llc

http://lascrucesmagazine.com/new-era-working-virtually-wild-wild-west-2

www.ingramcontent.com/pod-product-compliance
Lightning Source LLC
Chambersburg PA
CBHW031814190326
41518CB00006B/337